7

poets

4

days

1

book

7 poets
4 days
1 book

Marvin Bell

István László Geher

Ksenia Golubovich

Simone Inguanez

Christopher Merrill

Tomaž Šalamun

Dean Young

edited by
Christopher Merrill

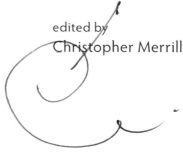

 Trinity University Press
San Antonio

Special thanks to the International Writing Program at the University of Iowa, which brought the poets together with the support of the Bureau of Educational and Cultural Affairs at the U.S. Department of State, the Ida Cordelia Beam Distinguished Visiting Professorships Program, and the Arts and Humanities Initiative from the Office of the Vice President for Research, and to Kecia Lynn, who provided cookies, coffee, pens and paper, and good cheer for this creative endeavor.

Published by Trinity University Press
San Antonio, Texas 78212

István László Geher's poems were translated by the poet and his father, István Géher; Simone Inguanez's poems were translated by Maria Grech Ganado; Tomaž Šalamun's poems were translated by the poet and Michael Taren.

Cover design by David Drummond
Book design by BookMatters, Berkeley

⊖ The paper used in this publication meets the minimum requirements of the American National Standard for Information Sciences—Permanence of Paper for Printed Library Materials, ANSI Z39.48-1992.

Library of Congress Cataloging-in-Publication Data
is available on file.

13 12 11 10 09 5 4 3 2 1

Printed in China

introduction

In October 2007, in a sunlit room at the University of Iowa, six poets—István László Geher from Hungary, Simone Inguanez from Malta, Tomaž Šalamun from Slovenia, Ksenia Golubovich from Russia, Marvin Bell and Dean Young from the United States—and I joined in an experiment designed to strengthen the bonds of friendship—and to make something new on the page. For four days, we wrote together in a spirit of exploration, creating a conversation in poetry, which crossed linguistic borders, aesthetic boundaries, and generational divides. *Seven Poets, Four Days, One Book* is the result of our collaboration.

We gathered around a long table in the library of Shambaugh House, headquarters of the International Writing Program, which brings writers from all over the world for residencies in Iowa City, and set to work. Our springboard was the definition of the word *union*, about which we wrote for thirty minutes, with the loosest formal imperative—fifteen lines, in any meter. Then we took turns reading our rough drafts aloud, not without some trepidation, and soon we were borrowing from one another's poems—words, phrases, images—to incorporate in our own poems in the next round of writing. By the end of the day we each had two poems to revise and notes for a third to be written overnight—the starting point for our next meeting. And so it went for three more days, building poem by poem, creating the polyphony of voices that resonates throughout these poems.

The French Surrealists provided models for our project. The poetic experiments that André Breton and his friends undertook between the two world wars yielded new ways of conceiving of literary value, predicated on chance operations. Automatic writing (writing in the absence of conscious control); exquisite corpse, wherein poets contribute lines to a group poem without knowing what their collaborators have written; collage and cut-up techniques—in these forms of serious play lay the seeds of our conversation. *The Magnetic Fields*, a book-length exercise in automatic writing by André Breton and Philippe Soupault, which was published in 1920; *The Immaculate Conception* (1930), a collection of prose poems by Breton and Paul Éluard, which they believed was written in a state of possession; *Slow Under Construction*, which Breton, Éluard, and René Char composed during a driving tour of southern France in 1930—these books inspired my decision to invite poets from around the world to dream up a sequence of poems together.

In his definitive *History of Surrealism* Maurice Nadeau notes the importance of collaboration for the French Surrealists, who "daily indulged in collective games and experiments that involved much more than killing time: the game of folded paper, the game of questions and answers, *cadavers exquis*, the game of truth and consequences, in which they achieved not only creations of which each would have been individually incapable, but a deepened knowledge of each man by all the others." Thus they discovered new means of tapping into the imagination. "The most magnificent doors," Breton and Éluard declared in *The Immaculate Conception*, "are those behind which the words: 'Open in the name of the law' are spoken." What they opened were the marvelous doors of the unconscious. And what they found in those rooms of desire—unsettling images, surprising juxtapositions of ideas, the marriage of dream and reality—

decisively shaped the art and literature of the twentieth century, altering the very ways in which we think about the human condition. From jump cuts in film to Jackson Pollock's action paintings to the non sequiturs of countless comedians—nearly everything that counts in the creative realm bears some trace of Surrealism.

But Nadeau was mistaken in his belief that the Surrealists were "the first to dare to write collective poems, eliminating thereby the role of the poet legislating from atop some Sinai, or even simply of the *littérateur* who too often supposes himself the sole author of what he writes." Long before the Surrealists, the tradition of the *renga* thrived in eighth-century Japan. The *renga* was a form that for hundreds of years brought poets together to write chains of poems. The most revered guest was invited to write the first stanza, the three-lined *hokku* (which subsequently evolved into the haiku), and thus set the tone for the lines that followed.

The Mexican Nobel laureate Octavio Paz, an admirer of the Surrealists, adapted the *renga* to an international context in 1969, when he invited poets from Britain, France, and Italy to join him in a hotel basement in Paris to create what he called "a place of meeting and opposition of different voices: a confluence." His collaborators were Charles Tomlinson, Jacques Roubaud, and Eduardo

Sanguineti, and their search for convergence between Eastern and Western literary traditions ("Joy underground," in Paz's memorable phrase) resulted in a suite of sonnets, dedicated to Breton, which in its mingling of voices gives rise to a new way of imagining poetic inspiration—not as the province solely of the gifted individual but as terrain that might be charted by kindred spirits.

Paz's reactions to this "game without adversaries," documented in his customarily lucid fashion in the introduction to *Renga: A Chain of Poems* (1971), include feelings of oppression, shame, voyeurism, and returning—all of which I experienced in the composition of our book. And I suspect that my fellow poets ran through the same gamut of emotions, beginning with what Paz identified as "a feeling of abandonment, rapidly changing into disquiet, then into aggressiveness." He continues:

⊚ The enemy is nobody, the anger involves nobody. One goes from humility to anger, from anger to humility: to write as well as one can, not in order to be better than the others, but in order to contribute to the elaboration of a text the aim of which is to represent neither me nor the others; to advance unarmed across the paper, to lose oneself in the act of writing, to be nobody and oneself at the same time. ⊚

Indeed the thrill of writing with others is that it allows one to experience the sensation of being simultaneously oneself and other: one definition of love.

For this book we adopted a version of drama's classical unities, gathering in the library each day at the same time, eager to embark on the next leg of the journey, fortified with cookies and coffee. From the first hour to the last, an air of expectancy filled the room, anxiety even, which in my case seemed to diminish as soon as I managed to put a word or two down on paper. Nor do I think that I am mistaken in believing that once underway we all pulled for the others to write from the depths of their being: "Success in Circuit lies," as Emily Dickinson observed.

Check your ego at the door—this was the order given to the musicians enlisted to record a song for Band Aid in 1985, the proceeds from which were donated to victims of famine in Ethiopia. And it is useful advice for any collaboration. Under the eyes of your friends, who hope not to embarrass themselves, you must surrender to your materials, and forgive yourself in advance for infelicities, clichés, and lapses in rhythm or phrasing. This is what distinguishes lively conversation, when we make light of our circumstances. A sense of humor is crucial, and we were blessed to have funny people in the room.

István, Simone, and Tomaž wrote in their native languages then read translations done on the fly. Ksenia switched back and forth between Russian and English. And at every turn Marvin, Dean, and I heard our mother tongue anew. The sun shone through the windows, and as we traded jokes and puns, crossed out words and added others, or gazed at the books on the shelves, following the meta-language of poetry to its sometimes zany conclusions, it felt as though we were writing our way into a different world: "Goodbye sky, aren't you tired of your war with the invisible?"

Marvin Bell, who in forty years of service to the Iowa Writers' Workshop had taught his students to surrender to their materials, says he "welcomed the sense of discovery and the unprogrammed expressions that art can create and which collaboration can but foster. . . .

◉ Our little band of poets half-escaped the daily wars to live in two worlds at once—or was it seven? Our seven planets did seem to chart their own solar system, in which we were subject to one another's force field. I was happy for it to be so and found myself embedding my reality in the sometimes surreality of our interplanetary union. I felt throughout the dialogue that poetry, again and again, had triumphed over theory. ◉

From his work as a translator of English poetry, István László Geher knew the transformative pleasures of attempting to render into one's own language the fruits of another's insight. From his time with our group, he learned that "assuming others' ways of thinking, shared emotions and images broadens the prospect of your own creative practice. . . .

◎ It inevitably redefines your preconceptions about your own way of writing, demolishing walls of solitude and building up new walls around a common union. You need walls to remain what you are, but rebuilding the limits with the help of other creative presences around will raise you to a new level of understanding. ◎

Russian poet Ksenia Golubovich recognizes the powerful roots of our shared energy:

◎ The residue I was left with, or could trap in my head, was something that could not belong to me nor did it fully belong to *anyone else*. It was truly a *common possession*, or—in an adolescent sense—the exciting possibility of stealing. You could take words from another person's mind and tongue under the very eyes of their owners. A thrill of theft met with a vague moment of self-sacrifice. *What I am now is you.* The fact that now "you" came from so many different tongues made that feeling even stronger. Truly a ritual suspension of the everyday—what the ancients celebrated in their orgies or saturnalias. A telepathy. ◉

Simone Inguanez, the first Maltese poet to participate in the International Writing Program, admits to having mixed feelings about the project, at least in the beginning:

◉ I felt greatly honored by the invitation to work with such a wonderful group of well-accomplished poets. On the other hand, I was quite unsure I could compose twelve good poems in four days—and in collaboration with writers I was effectively meeting for the first time in that same process of writing.

But it did not take long to realize that this conversation in poetry provided an excellent opportunity for invaluable exchange. Moreover, it offered a setting to write from a different standpoint. And so it was. I found myself traveling from my childhood to my womanhood, from my homeland to my newly found land, from myself to new personas, from a rather innocent voice to an increasingly sensuous voice . . . Such was the influence of the dynamics created in a short time within the group, which lives on in our works. It has been a singular experience. ◉

A wild encounter—this is how Tomaž Šalamun describes our sessions (and is indeed an apt description of his own poems):

◉ I've never written anything between 1:00 p.m. and 3:00 p.m. in my life. I've never written a poem if I was told to, either. I've never had to translate what I've done so quickly. I've never written anything sitting together with other poets. But Chris's infectious joy, the honor to be invited into such company, the idea that we would try to do what great masters did thirty years ago—this was too much to pass up. It was like being on a roller-coaster in a dark cave, experiencing an earthquake, hearing some strange laughter and shrieks from colleagues, exciting, enjoyable, but also really, really hard. After four days of doing this my bones ached, I limped (literally), my marrow was overused. It seems that those of us who had also to translate barely survived. But: we were happy, beaming. ◉

To which Dean Young, who called the experience crazy fun, adds:

◉ The writing of poetry, perhaps necessarily, is such a profoundly isolating act (even as it strains to break through that isolation) that those rare moments when it can be done in community are utterly exhilarating. We are used to being surrounded by others full of anxiety, but how splendid to be around others full of anxiety about writing poems! The flash predicament Chris (thank you, Chris!) had put us together in, all those blowing sparks, which for me meant misshaping something I misheard and copied down wrong from what my comrades in our incendiary cell read aloud, was inexhaustibly inspiring—there was no time to be exhausted! I hate to have to hurry in life, but in writing I'm always hurrying, not because I want to get it over with (although one of the joys of poetry is it's always over with—the line ends and ends and ends) but on to the next promise of revelation, headlong into possibilities of new musics. That early fall week wasn't the happiest time of my life, but in that room with that remarkable group of poets who guided themselves by stars different than mine, it was bliss to be alive. And, it must be noted, my hero, Tomaž Šalamun, was among us, and to be in a room with his volcanic, open, benign, operatic mouse-god spirit and mind, to be writing while he was writing, to listen to what he had just written, was one of the great thrills of my life. I miss our group, by now scattered back to where we belong and where we'll never belong. But here is the record of our time together braided like gold and giraffe tail, lava and sadness, worldly grit and hallucinatory provocations of song felt in the known and unknown of every language. ◉

For four days our give-and-take created high spirits—a buzzing that began with a single word: *union.*

Why *union?* At the suggestion of the Irish playwright Mike Finn, the International Writing Program had commissioned fourteen playwrights from every continent to produce ten-minute plays about that word—in one day. Their plays were finished just before we convened to write our first poems, and it occurred to me that *union* might prove to be a talismanic word for us as well. On the eve of our last session there was a staged reading of *Union,* which took us on an imaginative journey from Iowa to Ireland, from Russia to Singapore, from China to Iran, and all around the world. It must have affected our creative energies and worked to shape our book.

Polyphony may be the ultimate form of union, in which differences of generation and gender, language and history, vision and poetics, blend and swirl, now sinking into the depths of the imagination, now floating on a gossamer of faith in the possibility of a true exchange: a choir of voices cascading from one line to the next.

In his preface to *Slow Under Construction*, Éluard wrote: "The poet is the one who inspires much more than the one who is inspired." We hope that this book works in the same fashion: as a text that inspires more poetic collaborations, more convergences: another union.

Christopher Merrill

union · *noun*

1 uniting or the fact of being united

2 harmony or agreement

3 a marriage

4 a club or association formed by people with a common interest or purpose

5 a political unit consisting of a number of states or provinces with the same central government

6 the northern states of the United States in the Civil War

7 a fabric made of different yarns, typically cotton and linen or silk

ORIGIN Latin, "unity."

egység

◉ *wholeness or unit in Hungarian*

◉

Of this and that. The union of fabric and flesh. As when the bugler rose one night from a deep sleep, pulled on his fatigues, and left the regiment camped outside the walled city to wander through the desert until he came to a cave in which the scrolls had moldered and the bones of the divine shone intermittently. Tracer rounds lit a new route to the interior of the mud hut in which the patriarch of the family at prayer opened the holy book to the page on which nothing was written, and closed his eyes to chant above the din of artillery shells and the staccato of small arms fire. The quartermaster studied the neighborhood associations listed in the appendix of the report on the bridges destroyed in the last offensive, and counted backward from ten. A tune forgotten by the bugler echoed in the cave, like the words dissolving on the scroll. Five, four, three . . .

.
CM
.

◉

A single car horn eighth-note signals
a four-day union of seven who write.
A waterfall of tires on wet roadway
enters through a window. These connect.
I hear the silence. I usually hear the silence.
There is sound and no-sound in the paring
of an apple. In the thrust of an auto
when motion turns to scrap metal at the end.
One has also an urge to hear the unheard,
to see the invisible, smell the odorless,
touch the insubstantial and then to taste
the last ashes of an earth in flames
before it meets the sun. We are given to
this unity of nourishment and damnation
because we cook up words to cover silence.

.

M B

.

Union. Definitions

Two definitions arc unlucky. Numbers 6
And 5 (could barely get one in math)—both Failures:
Rich South masters of the slaves, poor North
Slave Slavic kingdom stretching to Kamchatka.
USSR . . . redemption for the word!
Ascend the steep ascent—"a club"
—Fourth definition—"formed by people
Of common interest" . . . Club? Common? Interest?
I call it war, and better rest with Poet
In his contemptuous, lonely Dive.
Then marriage? That is law, and law begets but law
Of private wars, economies of fear.
Then . . . harmony, the state of being . . . How?
O yes . . . Move on, move up, move closer . . . yes
That blushing union of the first encounter.

.
KG
.

◉

What kind of worm will now appear?
No idea. Will he understand the word
union? Will he lick it? Will he
explode it? I'd like you, animal, you'd
understand it. Because now my language
rips me like a cruel hooker. It leads
astray, thralls, fizzles and enslaves.
Worm! Be gentle! You can be
cheeky, saucy and *il terribile*, but
please, be also kind. We need you. We're
celebrating. IWP* was fucking great. It
gave a lot of light, huge joy to all of
us who rambled here around. Our
space which designates the word union.
OK, my little beast, will you cooperate?

.
TS
.

*International Writing Program

behind steamy windows everything's a blur

behind steamy windows, we drink cold coffee,
trying to pick up—everything's a blur:

the bunch of hippies sitting outside
sell junk—students leaf
through old pages of second-hand books
eyes down—men stoned already at first light
gesticulate and blab
with cracks in pavements—the smart
young man in his usual corner among them
reads loudly from the bible: *make ready the way
of the lord in the desert*—and low-lying
bewildered clouds flit by.

you tell me *time and empty space are beads
on a string* and you move your stool up and tell me
your life story, a rushed fairy tale
—till your face is reflected in the bottom of the cup.

.
S I
.

◉

Whatever lives, there is no place for desire.
The Sun would not burn if it desired to burn.
Its light would not scatter, but as quicksilver
Desire would condense. If we should not live.
Desire wouldn't be on the move, heads in half-light
Would protrude, halfway in desire.
And if I loved you, I could say, stay with me.
If you looked at me, there would be no urge on
    your face.
Each breath would then submerge
Back to the sigh of engendering, which never lives
But forces life, losing its roots on the move—
Imagine the wind as your mother or father,
On other bodies your life, recognizing.
What kind of moving power could be
Desire if no one was there for uniting?

.
I G
.

Isn't Being Upside Down the Real Game?

Hurt animal, don't you still love the myriad?
Myriad the burning ark, myriad your pop beads
popped. I love the narration of your life
taking longer than my life, more lasting than
its last ashes, a wetter waterfall than its worm.
I love your contaminates, a new red in the network,
new storm huffing to sea. I don't need the sea
to tell me whose sigh I sink back to, I see
the bubbles where it all went down, the surge
when it comes back up, hiccup, drunk licorice,
scent of brackish grasses, a faith of guesses.
I don't believe we'll ever truly part, it's just
we can't meet, too magnetic, too repulsive, warps
the day on the wrong warpath but the night,
shot peregrine, keeps splurging in throes.

.

DY

.

◉

Dean is your friend. He loves contamination.
Pirate, I call you pirate, my worm. Go and
eat. Strip the moon, strip the sun, spring the dark
mass. Creep on the meadow. Throw the luncheon
from the table. Grind it. Call your brothers.
After how many cubes, after how many cubes of
gold. Yours are mountains. Ours are leaves.
Every whirlpool has its price. What? You
want to bring your pink skin to Heaven? Do you
evaporate thunder? Will you be circular like a
drum? Will the birds nudge you apart? Only
women were free on the plain. They rode. With
light-blue shawls. Then we went to the southern
lands. Walked on the mountain, where there
were still some bones left from vultures.

.

T S

.

⊙

Open the book to the page where there is nothing
Written. Read it. I listen. I learn before you.
A voice needs an end, silence never does,
Half-hidden it speaks through the coverage.
That's why I have fallen in love
With your eyes, closed, even if wide open,
Practicing for death well in advance. Your gaze
Like foam on the water's face keeps
Lurking on the surface. Last time I had
Your palm in my hand, the lines on it
Were rivers creeping up from estuary
To spring. Everyone lives in reverse. Open
The book. I want to hear you, don't want to cling.
My lines are creeping through to your palm.

·
I G
·

Re-entry

Hello dots on the earth, I thought at first
you might be sickness. Goodbye sky,
aren't you tired of your war with the invisible?
Hello life in the river, I'm not the one
who'll undress you with questions. I'll use
my paws. Hey paws, what trouble have you
gotten into now? Do you always have to use
only the red crayon? Hello foliating union, road
that goes and goes, the closer I get the more those dots
look like what I should be running from,
measles, a faculty meeting. Why do we say
time's up when it's gone, everything else comes down.
What can you see inside a crow, tree? Church,
go fuck yourself. Šalamun moves among us.
This is radio Iowa City, anyone out there?

.
DY
.

variations on silence

silence—that's what i recall, mostly
: the biting silence—of your gaze
where i still keep vigil, waiting for thyme to bloom.

a white screen unfolds before me, slightly crinkled
    slightly patched

—and i'm there trembling
in my childhood hole, silent
in a block—that's given up even on itself;

—you scrub my small body, bent over
the plastic basin with its broken handle,
a big pot bubbling on the light-blue tower
of a kerosene stove with its black door
—how we peered from far to see the fire dance.

and i recall the silence, scared
of time passing, your bones—cracking

because that's what i think
it's the silence, that will stay—

·
S I
·

◉

Ah, that worm half inside desire
moves, yes, trailing a slime
of tears, an earthworks of eggs, blood
and tunnels. "Move on, move up," we tell it.
"You are our contamination." You can try
counting from five to three or three-two-one,
this worm will never reach the bottom
of your being. You might better imagine
the wind as your father and mother
than look back for your birth. Is it time yet
to speak of war, of the worm half outside
our better nature? I know we are wild, yet
we are more like the clam beneath the mud
than the heron in the pine. I see
the little bubbles, and I know where to dig.

M B

◉

Quicksilver, and a sliver in the seam
Of coal smoldering underground, and resin
Collected from the final totem pole
Carved for the anniversary of the war
On the invisible. What did you see
In the cruel hookah? A new red
For the fall fashion show, another network
To infiltrate before the spring offensive,
Words in an ancient script that no one read
Until the fire meandering through the earth
Had been extinguished. *Too late!* the model cried,
Slipping into an evening dress designed
For someone else. What happened to the silver
Mined by our enemies to pay their debts
To us? The totem pole swayed in the wind.

•
C M
•

◉

Think now that wind
Comes, saying: "Will you follow me?"
Touches what remains of your body—
A dead cricket in unknown arms—
(Sad children love dead things,
For dead things do not hurt.)
So that wind comes, half your desire,
As if to put you in the book
Where nothing's written but the sounds
Of pages turned by wind. "Will you?
Will you follow me? Through deserted streets
Of Moscow, and Budapest, and London,
Those cities—thieves of hope—the quicksilver
Of Time, trembling of old heart,
And then perhaps unite once I turn?"

.

KG

.

⊙

Will you follow me, will you stay with me,
if I make war on the invisible? Will you put to sea
if I journey to the ends of the earth,
or have you no need for the sea? I mean to pass
the first and final totems, the stained glass,
the gargoyles, icons, amulets and rosary vendors
on our way to the place that bent your back
and made you live in reverse, in pain
awaiting the end of pain. Old heart, come see
the bones left for vultures. I will strip the sun
so we can see in the dark. We can follow
the horizon, circular like a drum. I hold you
in the unknown arms of the unknown. And you,
you must wear the light-blue shawl I so love
that will keep its color when the sky stops.

.
M B
.

Beautiful Valley Rolls the Balls in the Barn

The glass case splashes.
The glass case is a wild fable.
To the polyps the sail pins on the
roebuck. The poor devil howls.
Silence never needs the same.
Silly mowing doesn't see
the mirror of the sun. Through
the hut the trees don't blow for-free-
and-why, but with intention
to put the sky to death. The eyes
of two great grandfathers are baked
into the flat cake. They smell each
other. The elephant washes his trunk
and his apron. Make me the spring
dark. It will resound like a cascade.

·

T S

·

◉

He was waiting for us on the veranda with a belly
Shaking the wine in its barrel. He wheezed, a half-closed
Valve. *Good you've come. I'll show you*
The house. Just dump the beverage in the kitchen.
His stopped nose faintly blurred his voice;
Some sweetish tact, like a bead,
Remained stuck in his throat all the time.
It was dark on the staircase. We were searching
For the light. He dropped something, his back turned
Bent, groping. He served nothing round. *My wife*
Has cancer. You have a pale face too like a cloud.
Did you split? Put money aside?
He stripped us, undressed with his questions.
As if God were stripping the sun and the moon,
A God who got bored with the sky.

IG

speech for the water-table-display attendant
at the mississippi river museum

steamboats, keelboats . . . everyone
lives on rivers, *where's your river going?*
row—
rain—drips, learns to row
becomes river, and you—pirate,
prepare for the cascade, the downfall of your death
see it roll in the current, toll of drums, warring
with ghosts of water waiting at some bend
        you do not know
see the bubbles rise and search
the sky, drinking the murky water
turning green, spitting it back
digging dizzy drunk, flaying
the rocks, drinking it back, even while
it strips both sun and moon, and drops you
—with a thunderclap

.
S I
.

◉

Silence stores a forgotten voice
within itself,
at its very bottom. Or voices
(like outer space) store music.
Strip bare the moon and sun
and stones—
all those silent, misused things
to find in them a worm—
that lonely voice, to bring
its thin pink skin
to Heaven.
You toil and toil,
we hear it deeper now.
In the depths of its pit. Inexpressible.
I see the bubbles and know where to dig.

·
KG
·

⊙

Strip the tones of every color, every shade
Of meaning, and tell the women in the light-blue shawls
To meet us on the plain, near the burial mound
Dug by the martyrs for a cause no one remembers.
Their names were not recorded in the Book of Books;
And if our elders deemed their sacrifice a waste
We praised their unarmed charge in the most lavish
    terms—
Albeit in the code we had devised to evade
The censor's heavy hand. Three moths! The leafless tree
On which they fed until the autumn winds began
Will bear new fruit next summer if the women find
Their way to us before the marching band arrives.

.
CM
.

għaqda

⊙ *union in Maltese*

The Plow Goes Through the World

My friends, the plow goes through the word,
laughter cleaved from slaughter, aster
from disaster, rot from erotics. Smoke comes
from the halo, maybe a benefit of mistranslation.
This morning waking: a slip, a spill, a slur
while the sky gave up its color yet somehow
we find each other. I don't believe in shouts,
don't believe in whispers heavy in fat air
but under dripping umbrellas we fall in love
like giraffes, like sopped sky rockets.
There's never one language for that. Poetry
is always cockeyed, obedient to only other,
what we whisper for, wish to be true, to woo
unto woe. Unsmother me my darkling divisible
words from other tongues.

.
DY
.

◉

Taking longer than your life will be my way to you
Yet, if I try, if only I try not
To say too much but rather listen
To the rustling of the leafless trees and be
Obedient. I don't
Believe we could just part.
As if catachresis parts a word.
Take my hand, let ghosts of the river
Enjoy us. Is it? Is it? Is it? Is it the
Day of the martyrs? Our first encounter
And everything reverses . . . verses . . . Do
Women find their way back home
Where hands hold hands, like the letter V,
A slip, a split, a sin, an error, a mistake
A poet leaves untouched, perplexing the translator?

.
K G
.

◉

Take care bridge, you'll break or
topple. *One has always to hear the
unheard to see the invisible.* Here, on
the fence, the bride. To the fish sacred
luster. I had it. It left. Will you wash your
hair? Will you bend your hair? *I know
we are wild, yet we are more like clams
beneath the mud.* With eyes, lampblack.
Hidden with wine. The brick, the growth,
shoes are swinging. Shoes are moving. Dean
reads. He has a red shirt. I see his hair. I
see his hair. I see a bunch of flowers. Boy,
I portray you sideways. In your hands you
hold the book with the dark cover and
there, toward the trees, the Russian girl.

.
T S
.

confession by the river

i must confess
i fell in love with the river
i threw off the sea's vastness
and i feel it—the weight—of guilt

i'm pressed to say
it's what solitude does to you
—it wrings your soul
you see the leaves drop outside your window
colored snow with three tips dripping
red—yellow—green,
so you have to throw the window open
secretly longing one might lose direction
and drift in

pray—the sky will never lose its color
when the river goes dark

.
S1
.

◉

She gave me her elbow to hook on to her.
Tired letter V. Together the two arms
would make a W. What she talked about
had a flavor of coffee. The lipstick on her mouth
was the color of leaves rotting in black dust.
I prayed the sky to keep its color.
Between the lips instead of speech
dog-smell of drenched November.
Her breast like the bread from yesterday.
She would keep asking me to decide.
Mostly about her. Where she should go. There
I could've told her to a place never to return.
I could've said it was a waste to see her.
My first piece of advice is that of an old-timer.
She's hardly looking at me. The W is dancing.

·
I G
·

◉

I ask of the ghostly only that it remain
after the steamboat has towed its wake away,
that it linger in the oil of the anointed,
and hover awhile above the bean fields.
"What are you seeing?" it asks me,
"Where is your river going?" The ghosting is more
than a lifetime, it goes on singing in the wash,
in the wind, and in fires that spy cameras,
from their warpath, record as red dots on the earth.
I ask only that the ghost of this war remain
after the martyrdom has turned into lavish celebrations
and leaflets. I want to ask the ghost
to depart before the marching bands arrive,
but the ghost, if it is a ghost, encoded, perplexed,
does not answer, saying only, "Good, you've come."

·

M B

·

◉

He wouldn't serve the ghosts, who had assembled
At dusk on the verandah, in dark suits
And soggy shoes, to drink up his *pastis*

And mark the progress of the funnel cloud
Approaching from the south. And he wouldn't light
A candle for the other one, the woman

Sprawled on the staircase in a Latin stole,
Fingering a strand of purple beads.
She never spoke to him. And who could blame her?

He was the master of the stagnant water
Trapped in the gutter of a Victorian house
About to be dismantled by the winds.

And he didn't know what to say. The train
Stopped at the last station in his heart.
The whistle blew. No one cried, *All aboard!*

.

CM

.

◉

We are all aboard. All faces known and numbered,
Humanity on its grand ship, "Aboard!"
The Ark of Fire drifting down the river
Of Memory and Future, angels stand
And mark true borders—countries, cages, homes.
Where do we sail to? I ask, like poor Job,
Who lost both memory and his good manners,
And only complains and wails and "won't"
Into the open sky—please change your color—
Be what you cannot be, be what I am,
His friends' true faces tinted with disgust.
And God attended him: "My child! Cast your glance
At the elephant that washes trunk and apron
In an endless river innocent above
All innocence. And claim the Ark of Fire!"

K G

In the Beginning Was Broken

When did it start? Before the glue
on the crystal, before the man spent
half a life blackening out a name and still
not finished, rust on the iron bridges
that cross from fog to fog. Probably mother
had something to do with it before
she herself was the farewell bride,
crushing a champagne flute, before
the orchids simmered to cinders.
Sleep, sky, between my lips, there's no
proper goodbye. On earth first you must
survive the ants then fill your mouth
with dusks. You must hold yourself
together and apart from the question Why
did it even start? It just did.

.
DY
.

i'll scribble you naked

man,
i'll scribble you naked
—on effigy mounds
under blue umbrellas, dripping;

i'll lay you down and leave you
in sacred patches, where clouds rest
when they're done, where incense blows,
not wind, where (it is said)
by the light of the drunken moon, branches
and leaves dance so close they can be heard
singing in tongues of warm wet soil

and i'll return at sunrise
expecting you—we'll give birth
to wild cherry blossoms.

·
S I
·

◉

Yellow moustache, standing out on the pier.
On his forearms a hair of reddish glow.
He needs beer to line his throat.
Fifty boats a day, thirst quenched by dust.
The hull becomes a tent over the head.
Scorched by the sun, freckles are sparkling.
Carries along the trestle, searches for cloth.

Awaken to the smell of oil that his mood filters,
Nails are getting brown, wilting cloves.
The crackle of the motorboat sounds
From inside his belly as congestion's bass tune.
He looks at women tired
As a bush being peed on
By a dog.

.

I G

.

Before the Attempt on My Life with Zarjica

The Orthodox chief used the wooden
leg, his real one was bitten off
by the Turk. *He cannot hide it.*
It doesn't matter, it doesn't
matter, we don't notice. I displayed:
the glue, the gooseberries,
the ferroconcrete, but only Andraž
made from this the crystal. His
sculptures in Novi Sad and my Sea
in Kranj. How many tons of dry shit,
how many things died. We had
dewy eyes, we folded like champs.
There were beehives on the left,
there were beehives on the right, it
smelled of bees, we had tenuous penises.

.

T S

.

◉

Goodbye, sky! Can you take a hint? The chisel
We used to carve out of the mountainside
Masks for the farewell party at the palace
Became in the stone mason's hands an anchor
For the ark propped on stilts outside the city.

Alas, the space we had reserved for you,
Near the stalls saved for the domestic help,
Was given to another courtier
Who promised to take care of the mourning doves.
Likewise the cabin promised to our children.

No maps for this, the captain told the surgeon
Hired for the first half of the journey—the rising
Waters, that is. The rain would not let up
Until a bolt of lightning struck the ark,
Which would not sail, in flames, toward the horizon.

.
CM
.

◉

I put the sky to bed. I didn't believe
the whispers, the fat air, the heavy night.
We had water, flashlights, pillows in the cellar.
I was exhausted. I sat with the gloves
and shovels as the tornado passed, watching
the ladder lean, the meters tick, gazing
at a light bulb as if it were money.
By one entrance or another, having dug deep
to a place of purple beads left by worms,
we may emerge again. Is this the surface?
Is it? Is it? Tonight will be one for
the Book of Books. As always, the poetry
lies untouched, perplexing the translator.
I put the sky to bed. I didn't believe
the whispers, the fat air, the heavy night.

.

M B

.

◉

The river's a moving bridge between the shores
That suddenly decided to converse
And verse each other, doubling into rhyme.
We put the sky to sleep and hope that will do.
Our cities built in euphony and meters—
Between the lips. Hear whispers that unite
Air to air and build the iron bridges.
But then comes rain, through thick dim air.
The sky awakes. It starts its ancient bit,
With Indian arrows, with Mongolian riding.
The Morse code of war. Space intrudes.
Prevails and dances hieroglyphs of passion.
And the river changes to the old bed.
Seduced, it floods the city. Like Helena.
Take care of the bridges. Bend your hair. Whisper.

.
KG
.

◉

Hey man!
The poet lives untouched.
Flies and ants looked like black currants.
Bells had oxen nailed.
Did they pour them away?
Did they haul them?
Did Tartars come?
Did I walk cautiously in dress shoes?
My father could rest on a log in the mountains.
We had a family friend Adler who also
climbed mountains. You're feverish, you
don't sleep enough. Does this water level also
look like silk in southern lands? Where did you
meet him that he rolled in leaves? Some had
prickles, others skylarks. Barrels rolled.

.
T S
.

⊙

I portray you sideways, standing at the fence.
Have lost your shadow. Your mouth is glittering.
Branches and leaves dance so close that
The filtered lights cut you to smithereens.
Your purse is a cube of ice sliding on fog.
You hold your hand as if freezing in advance.
Searching for cold you don't recognize,
As if hesitating between two feelings.
Black lead is sliding. Now you smile,
Not feeling the ice on your face.
Each lineament tense as if
You showed how I think.
The wrinkles on your temple shine,
Lines on frozen leaf in ice. Two
Of our dry promises change places.

.
I G
.

crosswise

you tell me how you spend days—staring
at the busy ants on the move
lines—spirals—circles
games of hide-and-seek—dances—
you tell me the world's forgotten you
apart from them.
and you lie on the ground, crosswise, waiting—
for them—to climb your arms, trudging heads down
up to your elbows—shoulders—your burning chest—
your heart stops.

sometimes they swarm all over you.
sometimes one might break ranks
—read your palm like an empty book
and scribble a little poem,
and your lips smile.

.
SI
.

◉

Sky stands for river when the cage is full
And the birds tuck their heads into their wings.
Farewell to the barge drifting toward the bridge
We called a bride until she whispered, *I do.*
We didn't. And the rest was history,

Or so we told the retired harbormaster,
Who was revising his life list to include
A kestrel from the southern latitudes,
Which had by all accounts never flown north
Until the glaciers in its homeland melted.

Coal dust swirled from the barge, coating the bridge
And sky. The forecast for the bride and the river:
Clouds moving in by dusk. The harbormaster,
Sketching the flight path of his latest find,
Ordered us to move along. And we did.

.
CM
.

◉

Job at the café recalls the orchid lei
on the bedpost, still fragrant in the dawn,
before the Book of Books. Job the sufferer
will soon be breaking his silence, telling
the seven of us, as the umbrellas close up
and the sky is reborn, where we are to go.
Job says we are to step around the snakes
lolling at midday, if we are climbing. And if
we are descending, we will wear wet suits
and walk the sea bottom. Job says we are free
to set fire to the ark, and to the story of the animals.
This is the same Job some say never existed
and others place at the side of Pharaoh,
but today we seven are the rabbis and we,
if we choose to, can take tea and ask him.

.

M B

.

Happy Hour

How do I love thee, let me count the strays,
I mean lays. Scratch that. Who are you anyway?
What pot of honey is hidden in your snake hole,
what black currents in your eyes? I think
that I shall never see or go fucking crazy if I do
again. Well, crazier. Burned fields of face-down photos,
grand acidic cities, grand tell-alls to ghosts,
glaciers of vodka, how should I know?
Once we were children in a garden.
Buy that? How about we got as far
as the padlock? The beehives were candled,
your thigh a soap-slide, we both had a family
friend who also cried mountains. Let's not
go back. Let's watch it burn, the thee in me.
Let's flee. Now can I have a drink?

.
DY
.

СОЮЗ

⊙ *union in Russian*

◉

Unsmother me, History, doubling into rhyme.
The barges drift, the sky and bees keep time,
and I am like the bride of the harbormaster
who sees in marriage a doubling of disaster.
Play hide-and-seek, if you must, my past.
Run sideways or circle. The future will not last.
Take care of the bridge, don't drink the glacier.
Look under the material, beneath erasure.
Unsmother me, History, doubling into rhyme—
your myths have been millennium's anodyne.
Good friends, the plow tilling our common table
upends the past. It turns the storied fable
of original sin upon its head. It's time.
Unsmother me now, before the coming cold.
I can't believe in whispers. I am old.

·
M B
·

◉

The bath attendant with wooden legs, as if standing
on a pulpit, gives out the keys. The smell of stale
towels, flash of rust in eyes when a padlock
creaks. Someone is rubbing himself so quickly
that the skin reddens. The foamy water starts
to flow as if to quench the thirst.

The attendant with wooden legs bites in
his moustache, enjoys the sight of a biceps.
Too many bodies in fever, the tiles are cold,
soap slides
from hands like slimy fish.

One should not come here every week.

The slopes of men's backs shine like tombs,
vertical stones without a script.
Each water closet is an altar,
a smoky sky is reborn in the steam.

·
I G
·

Springtime for Snowman

I don't understand the cicadas
in my throat, coal in my chest,
tiny mushrooms called death stars,
scar, scar, scar, all the current theories
declaring the end of meaning although
I don't know what meaning means other
than partaking of the general alarm,
skylark-prickled dawns, inevitability
of causing harm I'd rather not understand.
If my house is on fire, it's no news to me.
If the sinkhole ain't my confidante, I sure
ain't its windmill. No god? No sweat.
No hope? So what. I won't let the ice
on my face be wasted, won't mistake
its melting for tears.

•

D Y

•

violet

this batch of photos i'd taken of you still
smells of you. sometimes i come across them
and carry them to the kitchen table
put on the kettle, light a cigarette. *smoking
kills you slowly*—no hurry—
i go through them (slowly), one by one
between each puff and pause. there was a time
i'd carry them like the football cards from my childhood
to prove i'd met you—we must meet up
for me to give you the missing pieces of your past
—for you to connect.

lately, i chanced upon them, put them aside.
turned back and placed them face down
and, suddenly, they oozed sea water
—*violet.*

S I

◉

You said the world forgot you.
Big cities, crowds, people. I am an ant
That found your palm and scribbled a line
With hidden acid, made a slight addition
To the spirals, lines and circles of your skin.
To the patterns of your fate.
Your lips . . . "He cannot hide it!"
It's darkening. I had a vision
That toward the end of day you stood
Under the trees and looked at me.
Your suitcase like a cube of ice in fog.
Did we depart? Did the desert change our skin
Into the shining coats of giraffes,
God's grandest pets? Did the acid burn enough?
Well, smile a little, take your tea and ask him.

.

K G
.

◉

Sleep sky, between my legs. I took a wheelbarrow,
washed the words. I watched who was taking the
shower, who went to the shower. Students of
the Academy of Visual Arts in Ljubljana make their
models wear underwear. Obviously curators
invaded this place too. What dull monas!
Puffed up blockheads, thirty years of terror.
On Kawara and me were something else.
Michael Heizer and me were something else.
What luck to be saved by Ferlinghetti and my
instinct. And gracious women in Rome, too.
What deluxe pompous asses, I can't believe
this professional craze. Darlings, you're
entrapped in horrible dullness, already thirty
years producing vapid salons from Duchamps.

.
T S
.

◉

The beehives on the left were empty. Likewise
The blighted trees on the right side of the tracks,
The rowboats bobbing on the burning river.

When did this start? At the orchid festival,
Where the last pharaoh ordered Job to leave
His wife and children nothing in his will.

Job refused, though in truth his fortune was gone.
Also his health. And even his leather sandals
Which he had let Dean Young wear home one night,

Inspiring the poets in Oman to sing.
And so the pharaoh set fire to the river
Down which Job and his family would flee

With a single pot of honey. *Look for me
In the snake hole*, the prophet said, pinning
A flower behind his ear. *I'll always love you.*

.

CM

.

Atmospheric Pressure

At the bottom of every beauty,
there's Duchamp saying it's better
with the cracks. Every beauty has its leaks,
handcuffs, busted dolls, wounded owl, tank
of nitrous oxide. How far can anyone get
a finger inside anyone else consensually
anyway? Every beauty hurts but at least
Venus was the single god wounded at Troy
so score one for us. Still, it's a rout.
Beauty you make me want to shout eat stop
scream cluck rotate help I don't know what
be someone else salt a brown stone wolf-
howl telephone forest full of wriggling
baby Mozart? Reality is some sort of sweet
membrane, lick it right it rains.

DY

◉

Okay, I'll be an ant. A kind of ant.
I spent a lifetime blacking out a name
I could not see. It was an ant's name
for God. In worm trails, in clouds,
in fishing lines creasing the rivers where
rowboats bobbed in the oils, in sinkholes,
in snake holes, in the cracks of shoe leather,
I saw the words. But no God. I crawled
across photos on the floor. No God.
The world forgot me, but the skylark
practiced its song where I could hear it.
I was rolled in fallen leaves. I loved your
cautious walking, your honey. I loitered near
your wash stand. Purple and silk. But no God.

M B

◉

You don't sleep enough. Walking
in the park in leather shoes, the cinders
stuck between the leather and the sole.
Traveler's-joys like dustbowls on the branch
are falling on your nose. The answer
to the voice of cicadas is in your throat.
The question marks of squirrels' tails
open sentences among the trees.
You don't sleep enough. It is wind
instead of sleep that blows the place of
your hair. You can't believe in whispered tales.
Your wife has been taken to the hospital.
You go in a circle. Once, twice.
You can't believe in whispers. Stop
by the bench as the light stops among trees, on the bark.
You tie shoelaces. Like someone vomiting.

.
I G
.

Long Ago

Bullfinch, bullfinch, sap, bullfinch!
Smoke is coming from the halo.
With the lathe I ripped open the sky.
I crawl. He isn't you, isn't you, isn't him.
His neck is straight, a giraffe would curve it,
a giraffe would carry the luggage on the
railway station, it would run. We would touch
straps. We would touch straps with our finger
and burn. Houses lick each other and
move. They creak in knuckles. The flame
licks them from the inside, first the lions above
the door, finally the lions' eyes. Remember,
the snowflake dropped into my mouth.
You wanted it for the title page. I was standing in
Central Park. Curtis Harnack wrapped me in a shawl.

·

T S

·

◉

The whiskey barrel rolling toward the gorge
Lodged in the drying roots of a red cedar

Felled in the storm last night. The orchestra
Played through the hail clattering on the roof

Of the performance hall, the regulars
At the Hog's Head ordered another round

Before the lights went out, and the city council
Refused to entertain a resolution

Condemning poetry in public places.
But Rachel's baby shower was postponed

After her water broke. She always was
Ahead of us. *Bottoms up*, we cried.

CM

◉

Mother probably had something to do with it.
Where are you, mother? Not a question to answer.
My longing was a baby from the start
That had no one but me to soothe it.
To sense the dew of someone's presence
To feel that none will disappear
Into the cracks and crevices of the mind,
Which are as hurtful as those other tunnels
Into Where are you? universe of doubt.
Rilke said that Magdalena found in the desert
The only One to meet her endless passion
For endlessly giving herself away.
Away she gave and yet her gifts
Unwittingly resumed their course
Toward mind's perfection,
Begetting blessings where most she sinned.

.

KG

.

this morning

this morning, the air smells
of sonnets you scribbled
on my flesh, last night;

or of flowers
you left to drip
frozen petals, behind my door
—till the wind blew them indoors
like clots of blood;

or of kneaded bread—
you said snow on my face
tastes of brewed coffee.
you may cut bits of bread
from my breasts, for the road
i said
—you replied
don't let them sag,
take care.

.
S I
.

◉

I have seen the Word, but never God.
That was what he said after arriving from
Jerusalem. And I wanted to know what
it was to be seen in the Word. But he would just
look at me. He was grabbing the neck of the vase
with his long fingers like someone about to strangle
but gently. *There is no God in the eyes of people.*
Then in what would He be? I asked with slight anger.
I expected him to laugh. He was brooding instead.
Left alone the vase and touched my wrist. I thought
he was going to stroke me. His wisdom had
a touch of the sour. I felt sick
of him as of cheese. His two lips
were opening to shrivel. I'd rather
stop here. I didn't want an answer.

I G

◉

Dust rabbits, dust cats, dust balls near the washstand—
The strike had entered its ninth month, women
Handcuffed their husbands to the chain-link fence
Around the factory, and question marks
Were scattered through a periodic sentence
Which ended with the dreaded words: *you are*
Condemned to death by hanging. The prisoners
Began to cry. The union leadership
Advised them not to worry: anything
Could change the judge's mind—a mote of dust,
A rabbit's paw. *Your breasts,* they told their wives,
Your breasts will be my bread. Take care. Don't sag.

CM

◉

Now we are cooking with gas. Shadows nudge
dust bunnies. Death to the vapid salon! Long live
the salon of dusty millers and wine presses!
I myself like to grind some literary theories
into the grape sap to see if they are edible
when drunk. Duchamp's nude fell down the stairs
in pieces. She lost her sex appeal. Too flashy.
It's the quiet that makes the orgasm volcanic.
Okay, I didn't mean it. Just go on as you were,
leathered in belief. I'm a bald ant, a wriggling finger,
mouthfuls of silvery fishlets in butter. I had a friend
who cooked the morning's eggs. "You don't sleep
enough," she said, and gave me bread and bacon.
Well, I usually know when someone means me.
I move in the dark without eyes. A body of honey.

.

M B

.

◉

Dust rabbits cross my path, I like to watch
Their delicate moves. You don't believe in whispers?
You don't believe in words? Do you believe in squirrels?
They are quicksilver, or rather are
Like the quick chords of the clavecin played
By a six-year old Mozart. Wunderkind,
Celestial doll, God's angel (people say
Before you're seven paradise is quick).
How innocent, and how precise the movements!
What music's played on those streaming trunks
Of thorny apple trees, Iowa's guardians.
Dry, clandestine, delightful and endearing
And yet when Mozart grows, he will have
His *Requiem,* his *Don Giovanni*
To puncture a squirrel's path on his membrane.

•

KG

•

After This Night

In front of a thin plate with round stones.
You say the red pillar appears, the salt
moves. That the red flame breaks out if I
shove away. *Silence preserves itself at its*
very bottom. Such is the consecration
of rocks. To you, to you, water,
water between mirrors. You are the new
young prince. Confused. Not yet aware
you wetted the cosmos. You'll learn
gradually by paying levies. Janez Bernik
said about Andraž: break his beauty,
his trap is his beauty. The horse, the carriage,
the shawl took care of it. It was given
back to him from Hades. Beauty consumes
him calmly. Silk walls take the breath away.

TS

iowa

i know i brought with me both waves and wind.
i'm sure i hear them, when my window's ajar
with the crispy salt i know.
i draw the curtains—to watch the boats bob.

ever since yesterday,
in the forest:
there are prickly-pears
and carobs,
black olives,
crowfoot.

beside the river:
—together with his lamp
there's the guy who sells *imqaret.**
i smell his oil.

you tell me that
in the forest strange creatures live
—*what they brew is bewitched.*

.
S I
.

*a Maltese sweet

zveva

⊙ *union in Slovenian*

All at Once

There're dots on the earth now.
Dark trees on the red soil.
What do you see inside the cruel hooker?
It's about a weak guild, fluttering with
wings. It stands on the hill, with the
surface in its hand. White coloring matter,
soft grass. Deserts and large fields of
fertile shit. The chisel and wider verse.
The sawdust in the corner for litter. Until
I comes, who undresses. I anoint him
with oil. I spread the lid with my
palms, but not too much. I say, stupid
catachresis. He lies down and I
hatch and enjoy and give back power and
freshness to his bark because I carry it.

．
T S
．

◉

Six-year-old Mozart with his nose in his ear.
Mozart can write in handcuffs. He composes
the music of mushrooms overnight. He traps
the beauty of the new young prince
between the walls, inside mirrors. He alone
is perfect if you never cry. He plays
the clavier in white gloves. And why not?
Mozart writes the periodic tables of harmony.
We are all workers in Mozart's union.
The guard with the wooden leg has orders
to keep out Beethoven and shoot on sight
that internecine interloper, Igor S.
His mother was a hairdresser, the guard's.
They are whispering about him as they go to work.
Beauty consumes him calmly.

.
M B
.

◉

She could give you an apple
as if she had a dream to offer.
The single closed line on her palm
was the dead end of her will.
She had honey and apprehension
in her smile, and a vain longing
to remain young forever.
Her eyes were water between
mirrors, multiplied as if the double
beat of the waves were locked
in her face. Her lips were black
olives. If I gave her a kiss,
a grain of salt would hurt my lips.
She would never draw the curtain. Undressed
to the Sea, she lends it her shame.

.
I G
.

in the beginning

in the beginning, there were grapes.
then the word—words like cherries
and daily bread, and like water
—before it freezes
where a certain someone's indifferent glance . . .
and, with words, your eyes, a well of knives.
pleasure pain
the edges of thin lines.

i still dream
you're inside me
without knocking entering this temple
which waits for you—
and i say *don't lose your way*
in the dark and you smile—
you taste of honey.

S1

◉

They wrapped the wall in silk—bright bolts of blue
Unfurling in the wind—and dropped the keys
To the divided church into the well
In which each night the water turned to oil
And burned with a cool flame until the break of day.

The horses under the red pillar reared
On their hind legs when the carriage arrived,
Delivering another delegation
Of archaeologists from Jerusalem.
Scar, scar, scar, said the driver, sharpening

His knife against a whetstone excavated
Before the truce collapsed and the endless war
On the invisible resumed. The wall
Was darkening like unto the sky. A star
Rose in the East. We said, *Is that you, Venus?*

·
CM
·

◉

In the night of blind eyes
Blind
With gloom
With sadness
With the smoke of burnt oil
The oil of hope
Burnt in waste so many a night.
You are condemned
To passion.
Dead prisoners
In their bitter wisdom watch the living.
There's no God preserved in human eyes.
Silence preserves itself. We reached the bottom.
I stand—they watch . . .
In darkness any move can change the judge's mind.

.
K G
.

Half-Life

In darkness every murmur emerges
from a body of honey. Answers
are snatched from flames, from strange
creatures fed by hand. Music is a mushroom,
an argument between mirrors. Night
condemns us to another life,
that bottom line of the periodic table
where the elements last only nanoseconds.
I'm too sleepy to start over now,
too awake to believe this quicksilver dream.
Please be gentle as an isotope can be,
darling who undresses to disappear.
Nothing breaks down quicker than Dean
Youngium, the last atom before
the first layer of devils.

.
DY
.

night

night, lie beside me
—in this bed by the river.
rest your flesh, blow—
turn me into your image
—let me bear you
in my womb, it's splitting
i want to feel the stars
stir in me—liquid pebbles in a bowl
repeat my name, warm in my ears
among the trees, leaning barefoot to one side
—our side.
here also, nymphs appear when the moon
is full—still alien still withdrawn—
and we're their ghosts.

here, no one knows who we are.

.
SI
.

◉

Just imagine a mountain with
flames licking it from the inside.
He would always nag me like this.
His neck of a giraffe wriggling
with sympathy. With the face of a clown.
And if I imagine? Then you will be the image.
The furrows on his forhead promised
no small talk, dead serious. Humor
was planted outside of him, in the context.
He died as he lived, in front
of the mirror, watching to see if the image
would disappear before him. He left
no will. He wished to live in the moment
when getting forgotten forever.

.

I G

.

◉

Is that you, Venus, cracking your knuckles
in the bulrushes? Aren't you due somewhere up?
Okay, I'm a sap. I saw the hurt owl
hungry on his branch and I thought it you.
It isn't you. It's me. But in the dark,
a whoosh in the bush can trip you up
like Psyche, and bust you open like a boil.
Okay, I'm sorry again. It was a famous apple
made me like this. It was dream lines
in my palm convinced me I am alive.
What fun my fingers had being Mozart!
How I loved the sour taste and crumpled papers
each time I started over. And that owl.
It will be licking the entrails of a rabbit
by the time Venus leans down to see.

•

M B

•

◉

The broken ring of minds awoken from their music
Beauty has no place therefore it's all consuming,
The lion's eyes are glimmering through the things
The beauty broods upon. Let's pack the cherry pupils,
The olive lips, the honeycombs of smiles,
All sweets and tastes, the apples of the kisses,
The hands that played with white fish in the dark,
Green seas of eyes. Winter's coming.
Someone will take my luggage to the station.
The shadows in the sun play like giraffes,
But the light's too pale. Take care of your tongue.
It can get bitter in mid November—
All the sweetness gone, sobriety prevails.
Don't look at fire unless it's on a match.
Don't think of water unless in plastic.
Let's be plain: meet you on the title page.

.

KG

.

⊙

First grapes, then songbirds, then the leopard sleeping
In the tree above the newlyweds' Land Rover.
He dreams of wildebeests. She lies awake
Until first light, when it begins again—
The yearning, the singing. The leopard licks the cub
Of the baboon it ate for dinner. Sweetness,
Like hunger, is demanding, and desire
Is ravenous for light as well as flesh.
It's a matter of arithmetic:
One glass of red, one glass of white, and then
A washing machine—O broken beauty!—floods
The Serengeti Plain. A turboprop
Plummets toward the canyon in which the guerrillas
Plotting to kidnap a priest toast the pilot.
The groom stirs in his sleep. *Sweet dreams*, she tells him.

.

CM

.

We'll Calmly Swallow This

They don't know what they're doing.
Girls remain lying.
You're rabid.
The papyrus' breath.
When you tear yourself
away from the chain, do you
still sense saltiness? I passed the night
on the sieve. Below the grill there were
eyes and water. Little cloths with
which you mopped the tiger's
front, where are the temples from?
The poodle has built himself a wooden
shack and leveled it with his right
leg. I shudder in the bindweed.
The bindweed overgrew my shoulder.

.
T S
.

◉

Like a leopard sleeping on the tree
was the way he talked to people.
He was not one of them.
With his darkling desire he walked
the earth the way the predator rests.
In the inner darkness the prey
is other-worldy, he used his heart
like someone learning fear,
clumsy, fearing he was no good.
He would have woken to any noise
but life and death and hate and love
were silence for him. He waited
for the voice. His claws, drawn in,
spared time from tearing. The sleep
in his leopard's eyes grew towering.
Those mounting it could never reach the top.

.

I G

.

◉

The river flows ever so gently
Under the cement bridge at night. You stand
Upon a river rock to show me balance,
Then I—to show exuberance. The bridge—
A simple stretch of steadiness above
A sliding strip of water . . . "fit together"—
You say. I stand on rocks, you—on the shore
Touching the tips of my cold fingers—
I find it strange—your thought amazes me
And through amazement it begets a child
—a thought of steps and rocks and of the river
That crossed the bridge's heart, its darkening head
Under the lover's arm . . . Is that reality
Sweet music of the minds? Joining
Two half-believes we stand and move. We dance.

K G

the falling trees are falling trees

the falling trees are falling trees
in the long run—the first white hair
and my tummy rolls to peep
over my levi's—today my legs
tire of carrying me, why should it matter?
while you rubbed my back—hands pressing down,
leaving red burning trails, you ran out of breath—
now you pass your fingers through my hair
you rest your head on my naked breasts
and let your eyes close—sleep—
when you wake, take me to grow old with you
man, i won't forget—the taste of apples
in your kisses, and the dew in your sleepy eyes.

the four seasons are ours: we start with spring;
spring opens up; grows even lovelier
and at its ripest—

.
s1
.

What Would That Letter after Z Look Like

The last question was beyond anything
the class had studied. A morning storm
and by afternoon it's summer no more.
I was mistaken about the death of crows,
their shadows never die. I was mistaken
about honeycomb, it's not full of god.
Sometimes the only ending is abrupt but
the man will never finish blackening out
her name. It turns out the burning house
is Byzantium. The breakers rake the beach.
I promise the same promises as hail,
fallen and furious and melting to nothing,
same grit, my love. Goodbye on the wings
of a burr, goodbye. Now it's arithmetic.
Minus plus minus plus minus.

.

D Y

.

◎

Okay, one last bowl of stones for dinner
before we wake. *O broken beauty* whole
until the dawn. The statue David's of a piece
with the bones and entrails left for vultures,
if you never cry. Mozart is denial. Poetry
is denial. Beauty is denial. Union is fencing
behind which condos rise with good views.
Please forgive me my war criminals. And
the crooks who took away our soul. Let my
dream kidnap a bucket of Texas slime
and make a man of it. Am I to sleep deeply
by the river or beget beauty in the air
instead of hewing the trees? Here the forest
is a forest, and our dream a little Mozart playing
brilliantly for the grownups, don't you think?

.
M B
.

◉

Let's try…………………..
……………..What kind of…….
………bait……………………
…….will take us into the mouth?……
With little tails we'll …splash……
…eve…………………..devoured..
Mass…………………..
………………………….wall…..
………...grass……………………..
Is a troubadour an ……….eyeball?
………………….Hem the hearts
…………..…of the taken ones………….
………..We rule with bits into the forked
twig…………Enamel turns…………
yellow…………...Darkness is desire.

·
T S
·

◉

What bait did they use? Something from the last layer of devils? A banner dipped in oil? A frank exchange of opinions on the meaning of the word *union*? No one could agree on the level of armaments allowed in the treaty, and so we scrapped our plans to remove the fish ladders from the river choked with dams. Which inspired another revolutionary idea from the chef praised for his inventiveness—clam sauce without clams. True, we had neglected to register with the authorities, and the warrants issued for our arrest named you as an accomplice. Their hooks were everywhere—in the arguments for and against the moon, in the slaveholder's prayer. The fishmonger was keen to invite us home, even if we didn't speak his language, because we were willing to try anything recorded in the Book of Books. We knew that we would meet again—on the title page.

.

C M

.

about the authors

Marvin Bell's nineteen books of poetry and essays include *Mars Being Red*; *Rampant*; *Nightworks: Poems 1962–2000*; *The Book of the Dead Man*; and *Stars Which See, Stars Which Do Not See*. His literary honors include awards from the Academy of American Poets, the American Academy of Arts and Letters, *Poetry*, and the *American Poetry Review*; Guggenheim and NEA fellowships; and Senior Fulbright appointments to Yugoslavia and Australia. He is the creator of a poetic form known as the "dead man poem," for which he is both famous and infamous. Flannery O'Connor Professor of Letters Emeritus after forty years in the Iowa Writers' Workshop, he continues to teach for the low-residency M.F.A. program at Pacific University. He and his wife, Dorothy, divide their time between Iowa City, Iowa, and Port Townsend, Washington.

István László Geher has published six collections of poetry, including *Through Five Doors*, *Draught of Air*, and *The Fugue of Sand*. He has translated the poetry of Emily Dickinson, W. B. Yeats, James Joyce, Sylvia Plath, Ted Hughes, Owen Sheers, and many others. He works as an assistant professor of English and American literature in the Comparative Department of G. Károli Protestant University, where he is writing his dissertation on experimental prosody. In 1999 he participated in the Cambridge Writers' Conference, in 2004 he spent two weeks at the International Writing House in Rhodes, and in 2008 he was a fellow writer at the Schloss Solitude in Stuttgart for three months. His awards include the Móricz Zsigmond Literary Grant, the Radnóti Award for Poets, the Babits Literary Grant for translators, and the Zoltán Zelk Award for Poetry.

Ksenia Golubovich, who earned her Ph.D. from Moscow State University, is the author of the novel *Wishes Granted*, which was long-listed for the Russian Booker Prize; the travelogue *Serbian Parables*; and the poetry collection *Personae*. A new book of poems is forthcoming. She has translated many works of philosophy and prose, including Bruce Chatwin's *In Patagonia* and V. S. Naipaul's *Middle Passage*; written articles and reviews on philosophy, photography, literature, cinema, and museums; staged a production of *Waiting for Godot* at the Moscow Art Theater School; and given lectures on modernism at the university. Her weekly column "Pages from a Writer's Diary" appears in *Novaja Gazeta*, and she is editor-in-chief of Logos publishers, where she is creating a Russian edition of *Lettre International* and a Russian travelogue series.

Simone Inguanez was born in Malta in 1971 and raised in the maritime city of Cospicua. She is a graduate in law, criminology, and youth studies from the University of Malta, with a special interest in science, language, and art. She is the author of the poetry collections *Water, Fire, Earth, and I* and *Part Woman Part Child*. Her work, which has been published in several anthologies, aired on radio and television, set to music, and translated into eleven languages, is highly idiosyncratic, especially in its rhythms and tones—a poetry that is at once minimalist and intimate, focusing on everyday objects and Inguanez's innermost sensations. She has worked as an editor and translator, as well as a children's advocate and researcher, and has participated in many international festivals. She lives in the seaside village of Kalkara.

Christopher Merrill is the author of four collections of poetry, including *Brilliant Water* and *Watch Fire*; many edited volumes and translations, including *The Forgotten Language: Contemporary Poets and Nature*; and four books of nonfiction, most recently *Only the Nails Remain: Scenes from the Balkan Wars* and *Things of the Hidden God: Journey to the Holy Mountain.* His poetry and prose have been translated into more than twenty-five languages, and his journalism appears in numerous publications. His honors include a Chevalier in Arts and Letters from the French government. He is the book critic for the daily radio news program *The World* and directs the International Writing Program at the University of Iowa. He and his wife, violinist Lisa Gowdy-Merrill, are the parents of two daughters, Hannah and Abigail.

Tomaž Šalamun was born in 1941 to Slovenian parents in Zagreb, Croatia, but raised in Koper and Lbubljana, in Slovenia. Recognized as one of Central Europe's leading poets, he has published thirty-seven books, which have been translated into nineteen languages. His seven collections in English include *The Book for my Brother* and *Woods and Chalices.* Among his honors are the Prešeren Prize, the Jenko Prize, a Pushcart Prize, a Fulbright fellowship to Columbia University, the Festival Prize in Romania, the Altamarea Prize in Italy, a fellowship to the International Writing Program at the University of Iowa, and the European Prize from the town of Münster, Germany. He has served as cultural attaché to the Slovenian Consulate in New York and as a visiting professor at several American universities. He is married to the artist Metka Krašovec and has a daughter and a son.

Dean Young, who was born in 1955 in Columbia, Pennsylvania, is the author of numerous poetry collections, including *Design with X, First Course in Turbulence, Strike Anywhere, Skid,* which was a finalist for the Lenore Marshall Prize, *Primitive Mentor,* and *Elegy on Toy Piano,* which was a finalist for the Pulitzer Prize. His most recent book is *Embryoyo.* His poems appear in many publications, including the *American Poetry Review,* the *Paris Review,* and *Slate.* He has received fellowships from the John Simon Guggenheim Memorial Foundation and the National Endowment for the Arts, and has taught in the Iowa Writers' Workshop and the low-residency M.F.A. program at Warren Wilson College. He is the Livingston Chair of Poetry at the University of Texas. He has a cat named Keats and divides his time between Berkeley and Austin.